PORSCHE 993

ISBN 978-0-9571940-0-7

All rights reserved. No part of this publication may be reproduced, stored in a retrieval system, nor transmitted in any form without written permission from CP Press. It is subject to the CPDA 1988. Nor may any of the covers of any of our publications be used without permission, with the sole exception of for review in national monthly motoring magazines.

Published 2022

©CP Press

Contents

Porsche 993 Carrera	4
Porsche 993 Carrera 4	6
Porsche 993 Carrera 4S	13
Porsche 993 Carrera S	16
Porsche 993 Targa	20
Porsche 993 Turbo	24
Porsche 993 GT-2	28
Porsche 993 Transaxle and transmission and Gear Ratios	36
Porsche 993RS and RSR	42
Porsche 993	47
Porsche 993 Gallery	50
Porsche 993 Rarities	61
Porsche 993 Production numbers, Engine Types and Transmissions	66
Porsche 993 Targa and 993 Carrera 4S	79

The Porsche 993 remains for many the ultimate 911. The Porsche 993 was introduced in December 1993 and while it shared many components from the Porsche 964 that it replaced there is little similarity between the two cars to look at.

The shape of the Porsche 993 was the work of British designer Tony Hatter. It was a smoother and more rounded design than the preceding Porsche 964. The 993 model was 80 per cent new and it was also 20 per cent stiffer than the 964.

Biggest improvement of all on the 993 model was the rear suspension, which was largely based on the multi-link arrangement of the Porsche 928, and mounted to a subframe. It transformed the 911's handling and ride comfort was also vastly improved. The new body also meant new headlights and Porsche claimed the projector lenses that were fitted to the Porsche 993 produced fifty per cent more light than those of the Porsche 964.

The new 3.6-litre engine delivered 272 bhp and 243 lb ft of torque and is considered one of the best air-cooled 911 engines. The engine featured sequential, multi-point fuel injection and ignition, controlled by Bosch M2.10 engine management.

On the Porsche 993, Automatic Brake Differential (available only on the Carrera 4) prevented individual wheels from spinning under hard acceleration.

The Porsche 993 was incredibly popular from the very beginning. Twice as many C2's sold in 1994 as all the 964 models that sold in 1993. Porsche struggled to keep up with demand for the Porsche 993 until the Porsche 928 and 968 came to the end of production. ABD became standard on the Porsche 993 Carrera 4 controlling engine torque between the front and rear axles.

PERFORMANCE AND ECONOMY

In fourth gear the Porsche 993 Carrera goes from 10mph to 110mpg in 27.4 seconds. In third gear it can go from 30mph to 50mph in 4 seconds, while 60mph to 80mph takes just 3.3 seconds. It can do a standing quarter-mile in 13.8 seconds and is capable of 168mph. 30mph to 70mph through the gears takes 4.9 seconds.

If you drive the 993 hard you may dip to 19.8 miles per gallon, but with a restrained right foot the car is economical at around 25mph. The tank capacity is 71 litres.

ACCELERATION IN GEARS					
MPH	Top	5th	4th	3rd	2nd
10-30	—	9.4	7.5	4.9	3.4
20-40	10.9	7.2	5.5	4.2	3.0
30-50	9.2	6.6	5.3	4.0	2.7
40-60	8.7	6.3	5.2	3.9	2.5
50-70	8.8	6.4	4.9	3.6	—
60-80	9.2	6.2	4.6	3.6	—
70-90	10.0	6.2	4.6	—	—
80-100	11.2	6.2	4.5	—	—
90-110	11.2	6.2	5.1	—	—
100-120	11.4	6.4	—	—	—
120-140	14.4	—	—	—	—

PORSCHE 993 CARRERA 4

The 993 Cabriolet in Knightsbridge.

SIX-SPEED MANUAL TRANSMISSION TYPES

Transmission Type	Model Years	Model Application	Markets
G50-20	1994	Carrera Coupe, Carrera Cabriolet	Switzerland Austria
G50-20	1995 & 1996	Carrera Coupe, Carrera Cabriolet, Targa	USA, Switzerland Austria
G50-21	1994, 1995, 1996	Carrera Coupe, Carrera Cabriolet, Targa	Rest of World except Switzerland and Austria
G50-20	1997, 1998	Carrera Coupe, Carrera S Coupe Carrera Cabriolet, Targa	All but not Japan
G50-20	1997, 1998	Carrera Coupe, Carrera S Coupe Carrera Cabriolet, Targa	All but not Japan
G50-21	1997, 1998	Carrera Coupe, Carrera S Coupe Carrera Cabriolet, Targa	Japan only
G50-31 6 32	1995, 1996	Carrera RS Range	Rest of World except Switzerland
G50 - 33	1995, 1996	Carrera RS Range	Switzerland only
G50-53/54/80	1995, 1996, 1997, 1998	GT-2 Model Range	Rest of World

SIX-SPEED MANUAL TRANSMISSION TYPES

Transmission Type	Model Years	Model Application	Markets
G64-20	1995, 1996	Carrera 4 Coupe, Carrera 4S Coupe, Carrera 4 Cabriolet	USA, Switzerland Austria
G64-21	1995, 1996	Carrera 4 Coupe, Carrera 4S Coupe, Carrera 4 Cabriolet	Rest of World except Switzerland and Austria
G64-20	1997, 1998	Carrera 4 Coupe, Carrera 4S Coupe, Carrera 4 Cabriolet	All but not Japan
G64-21	1997, 1998	Carrera 4 Coupe, Carrera 4S Coupe, Carrera 4 Cabriolet	Japan only
G64-51	1995, 1996, 1997, 1998	993 Turbo models	All but not Taiwan
G64-52	1995, 1996, 1997, 1998	993 Turbo models	Taiwan only

ACCELERATION FROM REST

30mph	1.7 seconds
40mph	2.6 seconds
50mph	3.8 seconds
60mph	5.0 seconds
70mph	6.7 seconds
80mph	8.4 seconds
90mph	10.6 seconds
100mph	13.1 seconds

ACCELERATION IN GEARS

	6	5	4	3	2
20-40mph	11.1	7.5	5.6	4.1	2.8
30-50mph	9.5	6.7	5.3	3.9	2.4
40-60mph	9.3	6.8	5.3	3.9	2.6
50-70mph	9.8	7.1	5.2	3.6	—
60-80mph	10.5	7.2	4.9	3.3	—
70-90mph	11.8	7.1	4.7	3.6	—
80-100mph	12.7	6.9	4.7	—	—

SIX SPEED MANUAL GEARBOX

Ratios/mph per 1000mph

Gear	Ratio
1st	3.81/5.7
2nd	2.15/10.1
3rd	1.56/13.9
4th	1.24/17.4
5th	1.03/21.1
6th	0.82/26.4

Final Drive Ratio: 3.44 to 1

PORSCHE 993 CARRERA VERSUS CARRERA 4

	Carrera	Carrera 4
Weight:	1370kg	1420kg
0-30mph	1.9 seconds	1.9 seconds
0-50mph	4.1 seconds	4.1 seconds
0-70mph	7.0 seconds	7.3 seconds
0-100mph	13.0 seconds	13.8 seconds
0-120mph	19.4 seconds	21.1 seconds

PRICES WHEN MANUFACTURED

Year	Model	Variant	Price
1995	993	Carrera 4 Coupe	£53,187 (GB Pounds)
1995	993	Carrera 4 Cabriolet	£58,255 (GB Pounds)
1996	993	Carrera 4 Coupe	£53,187 (GB Pounds)
1996	993	Carrera 4S Coupe	£63,655 (GB Pounds)
1996	993	Carrera 4 Cabriolet	£58,255 (GB Pounds)
1997	993	Carrera 4 Coupe	69,100 (US Dollars)
1997	993	Carrera 4S Coupe	73,000 (US Dollars)
1997	993	Carrera 4 Cabriolet	78,350 (US Dollars)
1998	993	Carrera 4 Coupe	69,100 (US Dollars)
1998	993	Carrera 4S Coupe	73,000 (US Dollars)
1998	993	Carrera 4 Cabriolet	78,350 (US Dollars)

2,752 Porsche 993 Carrera 4S cars were made in 1997.
The Porsche 993 Carrera 4S was priced at $73,000 without tax, $32,000 cheaper than a 993 Turbo

Porsche 993S and 993 4S models had wide bodywork like the Turbo and 18-inch wheels covered the cars potent brakes.

SPECIFICATIONS

Capacity:	3600cc
Power:	285/6100 bhp/rpm
Torque:	251/5250 lb ft/rpm
Transmission:	Four-wheel drive
Front wheels and tyres:	8 x 18 225/40
Rear wheels and tyres:	10 x 18 285/30
Maximum speed:	169mph
0-50 mph	3.8 seconds
0-60 mph	5.2 seconds
0-70 mph	6.5 seconds
0-100 mph	13.2 seconds
0-120 mph	22.3 seconds
Price	£74,795

The Porsche 993 Carrera S seen here in Sloane Square. A total of 3370 were produced in 1997.

The Porsche 993 Carrera S has 17-inch wheels and the Turbo model body kit. Suspension is also lowered and the car cost £4,200 more than the 993 Carrera.

The Porsche Carrera S has stiff springs that lower the suspension by 10mm. Its split rear spoiler, along with steel grey inserts around the gear lever and handbrake plus Carrera S lettering in the rev-counter distinguish it.

For the 1996 model year the Porsche 993 Carrera S was launched. Inside the car was treated to a ball gear lever and steel grey trim.

Here can be seen the Carrera S logo on the Tachometer.

Porsche 993 Carrera S has a maximum speed of 168mph.

On the Porsche 993 Targa the roof consisted of two large blue-tinted glass panels. The front panel could be retracted under the rear panel by three electric motors. The design and fabrication of its roof was by Webasto.

The Porsche 993 Targa had 17-inch wheels with a five-spoke spilt-rim design.

ENGINE

Displacement:	3600cc
Bore & Stroke:	100mm x 76.4 mm
Compression ratio:	11.3 to 1
Horsepower:	282 bhp @ 6300 rpm
Torque:	250 lb-ft @ 5250 rpm
Maximum engine speed:	6800 rpm

DRIVETRAIN

6-speed manual transmission

Gear	Ratio	Overall Ratio	RPM	MPH
1st	3.82 to 1	13.14 to 1	6800	37
2nd	2.05 to 1	7.05 to 1	6800	68
3rd	1.41 to 1	4.85 to 1	6800	100
4th	1.12 to 1	3.85 to 1	6800	126
5th	0.93 to 1	3.20 to 1	6800	152
6th	0.78 to 1	2.68 to 1	6240	171

Final drive ratio: 3.44 to 1

ACCELERATION AND ECONOMY

0-30mph	1.8 seconds
0-40mph	2.8 seconds
0-50mph	4.0 seconds
0-60mph	5.2 seconds
0-70mph	6.7 seconds
0-80mph	8.5 seconds
0-90 mph	10.5 seconds
0-100mph	12.6 seconds

Curb Weight:	3200lb
Weight distribution:	41% front, 59% rear
Wheelbase:	89.5 inches
Length:	167.8 inches
Width:	68.3 inches
Height:	51.8 inches
Front Track:	55.3 inches
Rear Track:	58.0 inches

Porsche 996 Cabriolet and Porsche 993 Turbo

The Geneva Salon in March 1995 was to be the launch for the 993-based turbo. It had an M64/60 engine, a maximum 408bhp and 300kW at 5750rpm. For the first time in a 911 Turbo production car the drive was to all four wheels on the Porsche 993 Turbo.

ENGINE

Bore and Stroke:	100mm x 76.4mm
Displacement:	3608cc
Compression Ratio:	8.0 to 1
Main Bearings:	Five

TRANSMISSION

Low gear	3.818 to 1
2nd gear	2.150 to 1
3rd gear	1.625 to 1
4th gear	1.212 to 1
5th gear	0.973 to 1
Top gear	0.750 to 1
Reverse gear	2.857 to 1
Final drive ratio:	3.444 to 1

DIMENSIONS

Overall Length:	4260 mm
Overall Width:	1795 mm
Overall Height:	1315 mm
Wheelbase:	2272 mm
Front Track:	1411 mm
Rear Track:	1504 mm

993 Carrera Coupe	993-330
993 Carrera Coupe RHD	993-331
993 Carrera S Coupe	993-340
993 Carrera S Coupe RHD	993-341
993 Carrera 4 Coupe	993-130
993 Carrera 4 Coupe RHD	993-131
993 GT-2	993-380
993 GT-2 RHD	993-381
993 GT-2 Evo	993-380
993 GT-2 Evo RHD	993-381
993 Carrera RS	993-370
993 Carrera RS RHD	993-371
993 Carrera Targa	993-410
993 Carrera Targa RHD	993-411
993 Carrera 4S Coupe	993-140
993 Carrera 4S Coupe RHD	993-141

The Porsche 911 (993 GT-2) made its debut in February 1995 at the Daytona 24-Hour Race finishing in fourth place.

During the 1995 season it won its class in the SCCA World Challenge, the 1995 German ADAC GT Cup, the Japanese GT Championship and the Le Mans GT-2 Trophy. In the hands of the Konrad Motorsport team of Germany the 993 GT-2 was the winner of 1995 Mil Milhas Brasileiras, was first in its class in the 1995 Sebring 12- Hour Race, was second in the 1995 GT-2 class of the BPR GT-Series.

Again in the hands of the Konrad Motorsport team the Porsche 993 GT-2 was sixth in the GT-2 class of the 1996 BPR GT-Series, first overall at the 1997 Sebring 12-Hour Race, third in the Daytona 24-Hours and first overall in the Porsche Carrera Cup.

In 1998 the Porsche 993 GT-2 was first in its class at the Daytona 24-Hour (GT-2 Class) and first in the Sebring 24-Hour.

In 1999 the Porsche 911 (993) GT-2 finished on the podium at Hockenheim and Budapest in the FIA GT World Championship.

On the Porsche 993 GT-2

Wheels were 14-inch wide at the rear to deliver its 600 horsepower.

The 993 GT-2 took part in the Daytona 24-Hours on the 4th and 5th February 1995, finishing fourth overall. Chassis 0001 had been entered by Jochem Rohr.

As well as race versions of the 993 GT-2, Porsche in April 1998 offered twenty-five road versions of the 993 GT-2. The road models output at 450bhp was 6000rpm. Options for the 993 GT-2 included air-conditioning and electric windows.

It is thought only around 80 Porsche 993 GT-2's were made from 1995 to 1998.

The Porsche 993 GT-2 is a very rare car. In 1996 Porsche built 3841 Porsche 911 Turbos and 849 of the Carrera RS. However, in 1996 just 14 Porsche 993 GT-2's were made.

993 GT-2
SPECIFICATIONS

Cylinders:	6 Twin Turbo
Power to Weight:	360bhp/ton
Torque to Weight:	333lb ft/ton
Specific Output:	119bhp/litre
0-60mph:	3.9 seconds
Front Tyres:	225/40ZR18
Front Wheels:	8J x 18H2
Rear Tyres:	285/30ZR18
Rear Wheels:	10J x 18H2

Manual Transmission Gear Ratio's

1st Gear	3.818
2nd Gear	2.150
3rd Gear	1.560
4th Gear	1.212
5th Gear	0.973
6th Gear	0.750
Reverse Gear	2.857

Manual Transmission Type: M64/60R

Driving seat in the Porsche 993 GT-2 race car

This 993 GT-2 race car is left hand drive

"993 GT Racing" on the tail of this 993 GT-2 race car

Another 993 GT-2 race car can be seen above.

993 GT-2 SPECIFICATIONS

Bore & Stroke:	100mm x 76.4mm
Maximum Power:	430bhp @ 5750rpm
Maximum Torque:	535Nm (395lb/ft) at 4500rpm
Maximum Speed:	189mph
Weight:	1100kg (race version) 1290 (road version)
Price new:	£122,268 in 1996
Transmission:	Five-speed Type G50/21 Six-speed manual transmission. Single-mass lightweight flywheel ZF 40-65% limited slip differential.

SIX-SPEED MANUAL TRANSMISSION
FOR THE PORSCHE 993 GT-2

Transmission Type	Model Year	Car
G50-53	1995-1998	911 GT-2 road versions
G50-54	1995-1997	911 GT-2 Club Sport
G50-80	1998	911 GT-2 EVO racing car

On the 993 GT-2 doors were aluminium-skinned while on the 993 GT-2 EVO they were carbon-fibre skinned.

The Konrad Motorsport team in Germany raced 993 GT-2s. The car had much racing success which included:

1995 Season

Porsche 993 GT-2	First in class at Sebring 12-Hours
Porsche 993 GT-2	Second in GT-2 class BPR GT-Series

1996 Season

Porsche 993 GT-2	Sixth in GT-2 class BPR GT-Series.

1997 Season

Porsche 993 GT-2	First overall Sebring 12-Hours
Porsche 993 GT-2	First overall in Porsche Carrera Cup
Porsche 993 GT-2	Third at Daytona 24-Hours

1998 Season

Porsche 993 GT-2	First in class at Daytona 24-Hours
Porsche 993 GT-2	First overall Sebring

Porsche 993 Transaxle

The basic transaxle was the Type 950 or G50 originally introduced in 1987. However, a sixth ratio was added. This was placed in the extension at the forward end of the gearbox. This meant fifth and sixth gears and reverse were in the extension while first, second, third and fourth gears were in the main housing.

Gear ratios for the 993 Porsche were new:
first was at 3.818 to 1;
sixth was at 0.820 to 1;
Final drive was 3.667 to 1.

The 993 Porsche had a maximum speed of 168mph at the engines limit of 6,700rpm.

The G50-20 transmission was used in the 993 Carrera Coupe and Cabriolet of 1994, 1995 and 1996, the Targa of 1996, Carrera Coupe and S Coupe of 1997 and 1998 and the Carrera Cabriolet of 1997 and 1998.

Porsche 993 Manual Transmission

USES

The G50-21 transmission type was used in the Carrera Coupe and Cabriolet of 1994, 1996 and the 993 Targa of 1996. The G64-21 was used in the Carrera 4 Coupe and Carrera 4S Coupe of 1996 and the Carrera 4 Cabriolet.

The G50-30 transmission type was used in the 993 Carrera Cup of 1995 whilst the G50-31 transmission type was used in the 993 Carrera RS (Basic) of 1995 and 1996 with the G50-32 transmission being used in the 993 Carrera RS Clubsport of 1995 and 1996.

The G64-21 transmission type was used in the 993 Carrera 4 Coupe, Carrera 4S Coupe and Carrera 4 Cabriolet of 1997 and 1998.

The G64-51 transmission type was used in the 993 Turbo Coupe and Turbo S Coupe from 1995 to 1998. The same models destined for Taiwan used a G64-52 transmission.

Porsche 993 Carrera Coupes, Carrera S Coupes, Carrera Cabriolets and Carrera Targas from 1997 and 1998 and destined for Japan used a G50-21 transmission.

TIPTRONIC FOUR-SPEED TRANSMISSION GEAR RATIOS

Gear	A50/04	A50/05
1st gear	2.479 to 1	2.479 to 1
2nd gear	1.479 to 1	1.479 to 1
3rd gear	1.000 to 1	1.000 to 1
4th gear	0.728 to 1	0.728 to 1
Reverse	2.086 to 1	2.086 to 1
Final drive	3.667 to 1	3.556 to 1

Throughout the production of the 993 many different transmissions were used including eight different G50 series six-speed manuals, four different G64 series sixspeed manuals and four different A50 series four-speed automatics.

SIX SPEED MANUAL GEAR RATIOS

Transmission	G64/20	G64/21
1st gear	3.818 to 1	3.818 to 1
2nd gear	2.048 to 1	2.150 to 1
3rd gear	1.407 to 1	1.560 to 1
4th gear	1.118 to 1	1.242 to 1
5th gear	0.928 to 1	1.024 to 1
6th gear	0.775 to 1	0.820 to 1
Reverse	2.857 to 1	2.857 to 1
Final drive ratio	3.444 to 1	3.444 to 1

SIX SPEED MANUAL GEAR RATIOS

Transmission	G50/20	G50/21
1st gear	3.818 to 1	3.818 to 1
2nd gear	2.048 to 1	2.150 to 1
3rd gear	1.407 to 1	1.560 to 1
4th gear	1.118 to 1	1.242 to 1
5th gear	0.928 to 1	1.027 to 1
6th gear	0.775 to 1	0.820 to 1
Reverse	2.857 to 1	2.857 to 1

SIX SPEED MANUAL GEAR RATIOS

Transmission	G50/31	G50/32
1st gear	3.154 to 1	3.154 to 1
2nd gear	2.000 to 1	2.000 to 1
3rd gear	1.522 to 1	1.522 to 1
4th gear	1.242 to 1	1.241 to 1
5th gear	0.024 to 1	1.031 to 1
6th gear	0.821 to 1	0.829 to 1
Reverse	2.857 to 1	2.857 to 1

SIX SPEED MANUAL GEAR RATIOS

Transmission	G50/33	G50/53
1st gear	3.154 to 1	3.154 to 1
2nd gear	2.000 to 1	2.000 to 1
3rd gear	1.407 to 1	1.522 to 1
4th gear	1.118 to 1	1.241 to 1
5th gear	0.973 to 1	1.031 to 1
6th gear	0.821 to 1	0.829 to 1
Reverse	2.857 to 1	2.857 to 1

SIX SPEED MANUAL GEAR RATIOS

Transmission	G64/51	G64/52
1st gear	3.818 to 1	3.818 to 1
2nd gear	2.150 to 1	2.150 to 1
3rd gear	1.560 to 1	1.560 to 1
4th gear	1.212 to 1	1.212 to 1
5th gear	0.972 to 1	1.972 to 1
6th gear	0.750 to 1	0.750 to 1
Reverse	2.857 to 1	2.857 to 1
Final drive ratio	3.444 to 1	2.909 to 1

1995 Sebring 12 Hour	1st in GT-2 Class	Auberlen Slater Cogbill
1995 Paris 1000km	12th place overall	Herbert Asselborn Berndt Neutag
1996 Sebring 12 Hour	1st in GT-2 Class	Andy Pilgrim Will Pace Larry Schumacher
1996 Mosport 3 Hour	19th place overall	Rick Bye Richard Spenard
1999 Swedish GTR Championship	13th place overall	John O'Steen Will Pace
1999 Daytona 24 Hour	4th in GT-3 Class	Geoff Auberlen David Friedman Chris Miller
1999 Daytona 24 Hour	3rd in GT-3 Class	Patrick Huisman Darren Law Danny Marshall
1999 Daytona 24 Hour	2nd in GT-3 Class	Johnny Mowlem David Murry Joel Reiser
1999 Le Mans 24 Hour	21st place overall	Thierry Perrier Jean-Louis Ricci Michel Nourry

Steering wheel and dashboard of the 993 RS, the cabin of this car has no unnecessary trim

Porsche 993 RS

Engine:	3,746cc, 12v, air-cooled
Power:	300 bhp 2 6,500 rpm
Torque:	262 lb/ft @ 5,400 rpm
Transmission:	Rear-wheel drive, six-speed manual, limited-slip differential
Price new in 1995:	£65,245 (993 RS)
	£71,500 (993 RSR)
0-62 mph:	5 seconds
Maximum speed:	172 mph

The Porsche 993RS above is pictured at Brands Hatch.

It is estimated that 1,123 993 RSs were built and of these only about 45 were right-hand drive. The 993 RSR featured extensively in the 1994 Le Mans and about 100 of these cars were made. It is compared below to the 1973 RSR Porsche model.

	Porsche 2.8 RSR of 1973	**Porsche 993 RSR**
Engine:	Type 911/72	Type M64/80
Cubic Capacity:	2,806cc	3,746cc
Bore and Stroke:	92mm x 70.4mm	102mm x 76.4mm
Maximum Power:	300bhp @ 8000rpm	340bhp @ 7000rpm
Transmission:	Type 915 Five-speed	Type G50/32 Six-speed
Maximum Speed:	175mph	182mph

	Porsche 964 RS	**Porsche 993 RS**
Cubic Capacity:	3,806cc	3,746cc
Bore and Stroke:	100mm x 76.4mm	102mm x 76.4mm
Compression Ratio:	11.3 to 1	11.3 to 1
Maximum Power:	260bhp	300bhp
Unladen Weight:	1230kg	1279kg
Maximum Speed:	162mph	172mph

The Porsche 993 RSR seen here at Silverstone

Above can be seen the interior of the Porsche 993 RSR race car

MODEL YEAR 1994
(THE R PROGRAMME)

The basic shape of the 911 was changed for the first time in its history. Headlamps were mounted at a flatter angle, the front wings were wider and flatter, the bonnet was raised forty millimetres and there was increased luggage room. When it was introduced the 993 was initially available in coupe form.

    The 3.6 litre engine underwent radical redevelopment with a torsionally stiffer crankshaft, larger valves and rocker arms, lighter connecting rods, lighter pistons, and expanded intake passages. Maximum torque rose to 330Nm (243lb ft) at 5000rpm.

    The 'Rest of World' cars were given a short-geared six-speed manual transmission. Cars for the United States of America, Switzerland and Austria were made so that all gears from second onwards were higher. The power steering system was modified and there was a multi-link rear suspension that was mounted on a sub frame.

    The Porsche 993 Cabriolet became available in the spring of 1994. The Porsche Exclusive department offered a performance kit for the new 993 Carrera that boosted power to 285bhp at 6000rpm.

MODEL YEAR 1995
(THE S PROGRAMME)

Autumn 1994 saw the model range expanded with the introduction of the 993 Carrera 4 which was availiable as both a coupe and a cabriolet.

    In spring 1995 at the Geneva Show the 993 Turbo was introduced and this car had twin-turbo chargers. Additional new models were added that included the Porsche 993 Carrera RS and the 993 GT2 with these cars only being availiable in coupe form. Porsche Exclusive built fourteen 993 Cabriolets with turbocharged 3.6 boxer engines.

    The Porsche 993 Carrera 4 differed visually from the 993 Carrera in that it had white front indicator lenses, a continuous red light band at the rear and brake callipers were painted titanium. The Porsche 993 Carrera 4 was available only with manual transmission. The plate on top of the gear lever was also titanium-coloured on the Carrera 4.

The 993 Turbo had 60 millimetre wider rear bodywork and was fitted with a newly designed fixed rear spoiler painted in the same colour as the bodywork. The 993 Turbo had a 3.6 litre twin turbo engine that was equipped with two KKK type K-16 turbochargers. The engine had 300kW at 5750rpm, and a maximum torque of 540Nm was developed at 4500rpm.

The Porsche 993 Turbo was equipped with eighteen-inch hollow-spoke wheels, where the rim and centre were cast seperately. 8-inch wide rims at the front carried 225/40 ZR 18 type and the 10-inch rear wheels carried 285/30 ZR 18 tyres.

The 993 Carrera RS had front corner spoilers and a fixed flat rear wing all in body colour. The 993 Carrera RS could be ordered with the optional 'Club Sport' package with larger front and rear spoilers.

The 993 Carrera RS had lightweight construction that included an aluminium bonnet lid, thinner rear and side window glass, and no insulation material.

It had variable-length induction runners (Varioram System) with vacuum-operated sliders to change induction runner length.

On the 993 Carrera RS the valve train was reworked. Intake valve diameter was increased to 51,5 millimetres and exhaust valve diameter was increased to 43 millimetres. For endurance racing the Porsche 993 Carrera RS could be fitted with a 92-litre fuel tank.

The 993 Carrera had 18-inch 'Cup' wheels, 8-inch at the front with 225/40 ZR 18 tyres and 10-inch at the back with 265/35 ZR 18 tyres.

MODEL YEAR 1996
(THE T PROGRAMME)

The 3.6 litre engine were given a power boost to 285bhp (210kW) for this year. Joining the line-up were the 993 Targa with its glass roof and the Porsche 993 4S Coupe with wide bodywork.

Porsche Exclusive offered a 3.8 litre power unit with 355Nm (262lb ft) of torque at 5400rpm.

The Porsche 993 Carrera 4S was available only with a six-speed manual transmission and all-wheel drive. On the Carrera 4S suspension was lowered 10mm at the front and 20mm at the rear.

The 993 Targa had a glass roof which was a pre-assembled unit. It was later bolted and bounded to the body in final assembly. There were three glass elements to the glass roof and these were wind deflector, moving-roof section and rear window. The glass elements were made of green-tinted laminated safety glass.

MODEL YEAR 1997
(THE V PROGRAMME)

For 1997 the model range saw the arrival of the Porsche 993 Carrera S Coupe. For this year all Carrera models were given a higher-geared six-speed manual transmission that had only previously been available on cars going to the United States of America, Austria and Switzerland.

The Carrera S had a split inlet grill in the rear spoiler and the colour 'Vesuvio Metallic' was exclusive to the Carrera S.

The suspension of the Carrera S was lowered by 10 millimetres at the front and by 20 millimetres at the rear. The 993 Carrera S had 17-inch 'Cup' wheels as standard. 18-inch wheels from the 993 Turbo were also available as an option.

PRODUCTION FIGURES FOR 1997

993 Carrera Coupe	1775 cars
993 Targa	1807 cars
993 Carrera Cabriolet	3098 cars
993 Carrera S Coupe	3370 cars
993 Carrera 4S Coupe	2752 cars
993 Carrera 4 Coupe	379 cars
993 Carrera 4 Cabriolet	650 cars
993 Turbo Coupe	1775 cars
993 Turbo S Coupe	182 cars

993 Carrera S Specifications

Manual Transmission:	M64/21
TipTronic:	M64/22
Bore:	100mm
Stroke:	76.4mm
Compression Ratio:	11.3 to 1
Engine Output: (kW/hp)	210/85 @6100rpm
Engine Weight:	239kg

Excluding cars that were to the U.S.A., 1980 993 Targas were produced in 1996 and 1807 993 Targas were produced in 1997

993 TARGA			
Transmission Type:	G50/21	G50/20	A50/04
Transmission Ratios:			
1st Gear	3.818	3.181	2.479
2nd Gear	2.150	2.048	1.479
3rd Gear	1.560	1.407	1.000
4th Gear	1.242	1.118	0.728
5th Gear	1.027	0.921	
6th Gear	0.821	0.775	
Reverse Gear	2.857	2.857	2.086
Drive Ratio	3.444	3.444	3.667

Great view of a Porsche 993 Targa. This version of the 993 was launched at the 1995 IAA show in Frankfurt

Porsche 993 Carrera Cabriolet seen here in Notting Hill Gate

The Porsche 993 Carrera Cabriolet with the roof lowered. From 1995 the 911 Carrera 3.6 Cabriolet was available with an optional lowered suspension package.

The driving position of the Porsche 993 Carrera Cabriolet seen above.

Clear instrumentation of the 993 Carrera Cabriolet can be seen here.

93 Carrera Cabriolet showing the hood in lowered position.

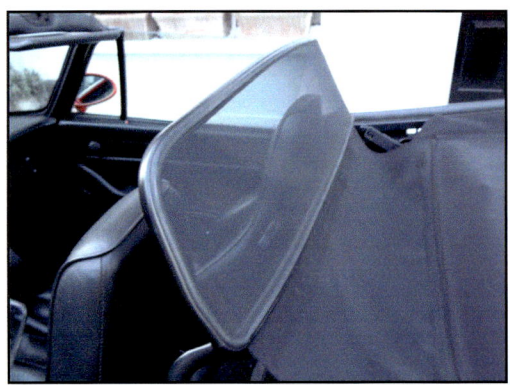

Wind deflector can be seen clearly here.

Another view of the lowered hood.

The Porsche 993 Carrera Cabriolet seen here in Sloane Square, London.

Another Porsche 993 Carrera Cabriolet seen here in High Street Kensington

993 Carrera 2 and 4 (Tiptronic)

Engine
Bore & Stroke: 100 x 76.4mm
Capacity: 3600cc
Compression Ratio: 11.3 to 1
Ignition and Injection: Bosche, DME, duel ignition
Steering: rack and pinion

Suspension
Front: MacPherson strut, coil spring, gas damper, arb
Rear: LSA system, coil spring, gas damper, arb

Wheels and Tyres
Front: 7J x 16 and 205/55ZR 16
Rear: 9J x 16 and 245/45ZR 16
Front Track: 1405mm
Rear Track: 1444mm

993 Carrera S and 4S (Tiptronic)

Engine
Bore & Stroke: 100 x 76.4mm
Capacity: 3600cc
Compression Ratio: 11.3 to 1
Ignition and Injection: Bosche, DME, duel ignition
Steering: rack and pinion

Suspension
Front: MacPherson strut, coil spring, gas damper, arb
Rear: LSA system, coil spring, gas damper, arb

Wheels and Tyres
Front: 7J x 17 and 205/50ZR 17
Rear: 9J x 16 and 255/40ZR 17

993 C4S
Front: 8J x 18 255/40ZR18
Rear: 10J x 18 285/30ZR18

The above photograph is the publicity shot for the Porsche 993 Targa. The 993 Targa was based on the topless 993 Cabriolet bodyshell. The car retained the classic lines of the coupe which previous Targa's had failed to do. The Porsche 993 Targa was introduced to benefit the market in the United States of America, where there were fears about cabriolets on safety grounds. Targa's command £3000 to £4000 more than Coupes.

The Porsche 993 Turbo S was a Porsche Exclusiv department product and featured two larger K-24 turbochargers. On the Porsche 993 Turbo S the wheels had a matt finish and not a gloss one

The Porsche 993 Speedster is the rarest of all the 993 models and a single narrow body speedster was built in 1995 and presented to Ferdinand Porsche on his 60th birthday

The Porsche 993 Speedster needed special parts that no other model or version used so it would be more costly to produce and so Porsche senior management decided not to go ahead with it.

Seven Porsche 993 Speedsters were built using the 993 Carrera Cabriolet chassis as a base.

Driving position of the Porsche 993 Speedster

Seats of the 993 Speedster are finished in leather

Boot badging shows that this is the 993 Speedster

Model Years	Model	Number Built
1994, 1995	Carrera Coupe	14,541
1994, 1995	Carrera Cabriolet	7,750
1994, 1995	Carrera Coupe Cup	90
1994 to 1998	Carrera RSR	374
1995	Carrera 4 Coupe	2884
1995	Carrera 4 Cabriolet	1284
1995	Carrera Cabriolet Turbo	14
1995	Turbo Coupe	19
1995, 1996	Carrera RS Coupe	1014
1996, 1997	GT-2 and GTR-2	234
1996	Speedster Narrow Body	1
1996 - 1998	Turbo Coupe	5959
1996 - 1998	Carrera Coupe	9878
1996 - 1998	Carrera Cabriolet	7769
1996 - 1998	Carrera 4 Coupe	1860
1996 - 1998	Carrera 4 Cabriolet	1138
1996 - 1998	Targa	4583
1996 - 1998	Carrera 4S Coupe	6948
1996 - 1998	Carrera S Coupe	4482
1997	Speedster Wide Body	6
1997, 1998	Turbo S Coupe	336
1998	GT-2 Evo	34

Carrera 993

Engine Type

Manual Transmission:	M64/05
Tiptronic:	M64/06
Bore:	100mm
Stroke:	76.4mm
Displacement:	3600cc
Compression Ratio:	11.3 to 1
Engine Output:	200KW @6100rpm
Torque:	330Nm @5000rpm
Output per Litre:	55.6KW/L
Maximum Engine Speed:	6700rpm

Carrera 993

Manual Transmission G50/21

Gear Ratio's

1st Gear:	3.818
2nd Gear:	2.15
3rd Gear:	1.56
4th Gear:	1.242
5th Gear:	1.027
6th Gear:	0.820
Reverse Gear:	2.857
Final Drive:	3.444
Gearbox Weight:	66Kg

Carrera 993

Tiptronic A50/04

Gear Ratio's	
1st Gear:	2.479
2nd Gear:	1.479
3rd Gear:	1.000
4th Gear:	0.728
Reverse Gear:	2.086
Final Drive:	3.667
Gearbox Weight::	105Kg

Dimensions

Length:	4245mm
Width:	1735mm
Height:	1300mm
Wheelbase:	2272mm
Front Track:	1405mm
Rear Track:	1444mm

Maximum Speed

Manual Transmission:	270 Km/h
Tiptronic:	265 Km/h

Acceleration (0-60mph)

Manual Transmission:	5.6 seconds
Tiptronic:	6.6 seconds

Engine Type			
	Carrera 993	**Carrera 4 993**	**Carrera RS 993**
Manual Transmission:	M64/05	M64/05	M64/05
Tiptronic:	M64/06	-----	-----
Bore:	100mm	100mm	102mm
Stroke:	76.4mm	76.4mm	76.4mm
Displacement:	3600cc	3600cc	3746cc
Compression Ratio:	11.3 to 1	11.3 to 1	11.3 to 1
Engine Output (kW):	200@6100rpm	200@6100rpm	221@6500rpm
Torque (Nm):	330@5000rpm	330@5000rpm	355@5400rpm
Output Per Litre (kW/L):	55.6	55.6	59
Maximum Engine Speed:	6700rpm	6700rpm	6840rpm

Chassis Numbers

WP0ZZZ99ZSS310001 to WP0ZZZ99ZSS319000
Rest of World, Carrera or Carrera 4 Coupe

WP0ZZZ99ZSS330001 to WP0ZZZ99ZSS339000
Rest of World, 911 Carrera or Carrera 4 Cabriolet

WP0ZZZ99ZSS390001 to WP0ZZZ99ZSS390400
Rest of World, 911 Carrera RS

WP0AB299CSS310001 to WP0AB299CSS315000
USA/CDN, 911 Carrera or Carrera 4 Coupe

WP0CB299CSS36001 to WP0CB299CSS365000
USA/CDN, 911 Carrera or Carrera 4 Cabriolet

	Engine Type		
	Carrera 993	**Carrera 4 993**	**Carrera 4S 993**
Manual Transmission:	M64/05	M64/05	M64/21
Tiptronic:	M64/06	-----	-----
Bore:	100mm	100mm	102mm
Stroke:	76.4mm	76.4mm	76.4mm
Displacement:	3600cc	3600cc	3600cc
Compression Ratio:	11.3 to 1	11.3 to 1	11.3 to 1
Engine Output (kW):	210@6100rpm	210@6100rpm	210@6100rpm
Torque (Nm):	340@5250rpm	340@5250rpm	340@5250rpm
Output Per Litre (kW/L):	58.3	58.3	58.3
Maximum Engine Speed:	6700rpm	6700rpm	6700rpm

	Engine Type	
	Carrera RS 993	**Turbo 993**
Manual Transmission:	M64/20	M64/60
Tiptronic:	-----	-----
Bore:	102mm	100mm
Stroke:	76.4mm	76.4mm
Displacement:	3746cc	3600cc
Compression Ratio:	11.3 to 1	8.0 to 1
Engine Output (kW):	221@6500rpm	300@5750rpm
Torque (Nm):	355@5400rpm	540@4500rpm
Output Per Litre (kW/L):	59.0	83.3
Maximum Engine Speed:	6840rpm	6720rpm

	Carrera 993	Carrera 4 993	Carrera 4S 993
Manual Transmission:	G50/21		
Gear Ratio's			
1st Gear:	3.818	3.818	3.818
2nd Gear:	2.150	2.150	2.150
3rd Gear:	1.560	1.560	1.560
4th Gear:	1.242	1.242	1.242
5th Gear:	1.024	1.024	1.024
6th Gear:	0.820	0.820	0.820
Reverse Gear:	2.857	2.857	2.857

	Carrera RS 993	Turbo 993
Manual Transmission		
Gear Ratio's		
1st Gear:	3.154	3.818
2nd Gear:	2.000	2.150
3rd Gear:	1.522	1.50
4th Gear:	1.242	1.212
5th Gear:	1.024	0.937
6th Gear:	0.750	0.750
Reverse Gear:	2.857	2.857

Chassis Numbers

WP0ZAZ99ZTS390001 to WP0ZAZ99ZTS390400
Rest of World, 911 Carrera RS

WP0AB299CTS320001 to WP0AB299CTS329000
USA/CDN, 911 Carrera or Carrera 4 Coupe

WP0DA299CTS385001 to WP0DA299CTS389000
USA/CDN, 911 Carrera or Carrera 4 Targa

WP0CB299CTS340001 to WP0CB299CTS349000
USA/CDN, 911 Carrera or Carrera 4 Cabriolet

WP0AC299CTS375001 to WP0AC299CTS376000
USA/CDN Turbo 3.6

	Carrera 993	Carrera 4 993	Carrera 4S 993
Maximum Speed			
Manual Transmission:	275Km/h	275Km/h	270Km/h
Tiptronic:	270Km/h		
Acceleration (0-62mph)			
Manual Transmission:	5.4 seconds	5.3 seconds	5.3 seconds
Tiptronic:	6.4 seconds		

Chassis Numbers

WP0ZZZ99ZTS310001 to WP0ZZZ99ZTS319000
Rest of World, 911 Carrera or Carrera 4 Coupe

WP0ZZZ99ZTS380001 to WP0ZZZ99ZTS385000
Rest of World, 911 Carrera or Carrera 4 Targa

WP0ZZZ99ZTS330001 to WP0ZZZ99ZTS339000
Rest of World, 911 Carrera or Carrera 4 Cabriolet

WP0ZAZ99ZTS370001 to WP0ZAZ99ZTS373000
Rest of World, 911 Turbo Coupe

	Engine Type		
	Carrera 993	**Carrera S 993**	**Carrera 4 993**
Manual Transmission:	M64/21	M64/21	M64/21
Tiptronic:	M64/22	M64/22	-----
Bore:	100mm	100mm	102mm
Stroke:	76.4mm	76.4mm	76.4mm
Displacement:	3600cc	3600cc	3600cc
Compression Ratio:	11.3 to 1	11.3 to 1	11.3 to 1
Engine Output (kW):	210@6100rpm	210@6100rpm	210@6100rpm
Torque (Nm):	340@5250rpm	340@5250rpm	340@5250rpm
Output Per Litre (kW/L):	58.3	58.3	58.3
Maximum Engine Speed:	6700rpm	6700rpm	6700rpm

	Engine Type	
	Carrera 4S 993	**Turbo 993**
Manual Transmission:	M64/21	M64/60
Tiptronic:	-----	-----
Bore:	100mm	100mm
Stroke:	76.4mm	76.4mm
Displacement:	3600cc	3600cc
Compression Ratio:	11.3 to 1	8.0 to 1
Engine Output (kW):	210@6100rpm	300@5750rpm
Torque (Nm):	340@5250rpm	540@4500rpm
Output Per Litre (kW/L):	58.3	83.3
Maximum Engine Speed:	6700rpm	6720rpm

	Carrera 993	Carrera S 993	Carrera 4S 993
Manual Transmission:	G50/20	G50/20	G64/20
Gear Ratio's			
1st Gear:	3.818	3.818	3.818
2nd Gear:	2.048	2.048	2.048
3rd Gear:	1.407	1.407	1.407
4th Gear:	1.118	1.118	1.118
5th Gear:	0.928	0.928	0.928
6th Gear:	0.775	0.775	0.775
Reverse Gear:	2.857	2.857	2.857

	Carrera 4S 993	Turbo 993
Manual Transmission	G64/20	G64/51
Gear Ratio's		
1st Gear:	3.818	3.818
2nd Gear:	2.048	2.150
3rd Gear:	1.407	1.560
4th Gear:	1.118	1.212
5th Gear:	0.928	0.937
6th Gear:	0.775	0.750
Reverse Gear:	2.857	2.857

	Carrera 993	Carrera S 993
Tiptronic	A50/04	A50/04
Gear Ratio's		
1st Gear:	2.479	2.479
2nd Gear:	1.479	1.479
3rd Gear:	1.000	1.000
4th Gear:	0.728	0.728
Reverse Gear:	2.086	2.086
Final Drive Ratio:	3.667	3.667

Chassis Numbers

WP0ZZZ99ZVS310001 to WP0ZZZ99ZVS319000
Rest of World, 911 Carrera or Carrera 4 Coupe

WP0ZZZ99ZVS330001 to WP0ZZZ99ZVS339000
Rest of World, 911 Cabriolet

WP0ZZZ99ZVS380001 to WP0ZZZ99ZVS385000
Rest of World, 911 Targa

WP0ZZZ99ZVS370001 to WP0ZZZ99ZVS373000
Rest of World, 911 Turbo 3.6 Coupe

WP0AA299CVS320001 to WP0AA299CVS329000
USA/CDN, 911Carrera or Carrera 4 Coupe

WP0CA299CVS340001 to WP0CA299CVS349000
USA/CDN, 911Carrera or Carrera 4 Cabriolet

WP0DA299CVS385001 to WP0DA299CVS389000
USA/CDN, 911 Targa

WP0AC299CVS370001 to WP0AC299CVS375000
USA/CDN, 911 Turbo 3.6 Coupe

	Engine Type		
	Carrera 993	Carrera 4S 993	Turbo 3.6 993
Manual Transmission:	M64/21	M64/21	M64/60
Tiptronic:	M64/22	-----	-----
Bore:	100mm	100mm	100mm
Stroke:	76.4mm	76.4mm	76.4mm
Displacement:	3600cc	3600cc	3600cc
Compression Ratio:	11.3 to 1	11.3 to 1	8.0 to 1
Engine Output (kW):	210@6100rpm	210@6100rpm	300@5750rpm
Torque (Nm):	340@5250rpm	340@5250rpm	540@4500rpm
Output Per Litre (kW/L):	58.3	58.3	83.3
Maximum Engine Speed:	6700rpm	6700rpm	6720rpm

	Carrera 993	Carrera 4S 993	Turbo 3.6 993
Manual Transmission Gear Ratio's			
1st Gear:	3.818	3.818	3.818
2nd Gear:	2.048	2.048	2.150
3rd Gear:	1.407	1.407	1.560
4th Gear:	1.118	1.118	1.212
5th Gear:	0.929	0.929	0.937
6th Gear:	0.775	0.775	0.750
Reverse Gear:	2.857	2.857	2.857

	Carrera 993	Carrera 4S 993	Turbo 3.6 993
Dimensions			
Length:	4245mm	4245mm	4245mm
Width:	1795mm	1795mm	1795mm
Height:	1285mm	1285mm	1285mm
Drag Coefficient:	0.34cd	0.34cd	0.34cd

Chassis Numbers

WP0ZZZ99ZWS310001   993 Coupe RoW

WP0AA299CWS320001   993 Coupe USA/CDN

WP0ZZZ99ZWS330001   993 Cabriolet RoW

WP0CA299CWS340001   993 Cabriolet USA/CDN

WP0ZZZ99ZWS380001   993 Targa RoW

WP0DA299CWS385001   993 Targa USA/CDN

WP0AC299CWS375001   993 Turbo 3.6 Coupe USA/CDN

WP0ZZZ99ZWS393001   993 Turbo 3.6 GTR

Above and below - press photographs of the Porsche 993 Targa and Porsche 993 Carrera 4S

Other Porsche Titles

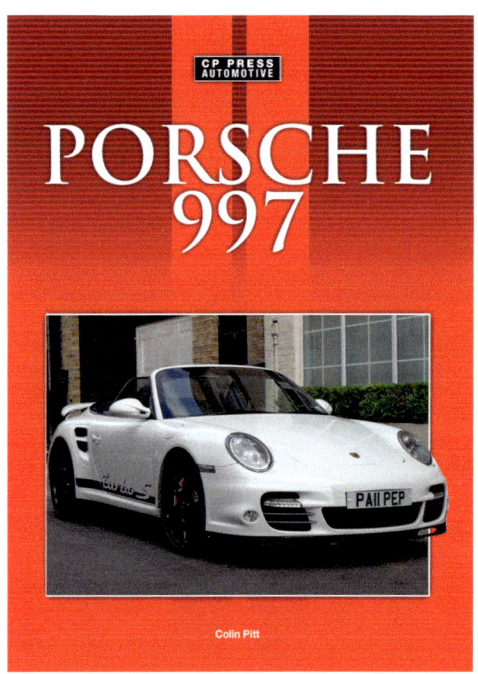

Porsche 997

£14.99

The Porsche 997 first appeared in 2004. In its first year 1464 Porsche 997 Carrera's were produced along with 1917 Carrera S models.

This book looks at all the variants including the 997 Targa and Targa 4S, the 997 Turbo and Turbo S, Carrera and Carrera 4S, 997 GT3 RS and 997 GT2 RS along with the Porsche 997 GTS.

Production figures and chassis numbers are also included in this new hardback edition.

- **96 pages hardback**
- **255 x 195mm**
- **152 colour & b/w illustrations**
- **ISBN 978-1-910241-61-5**

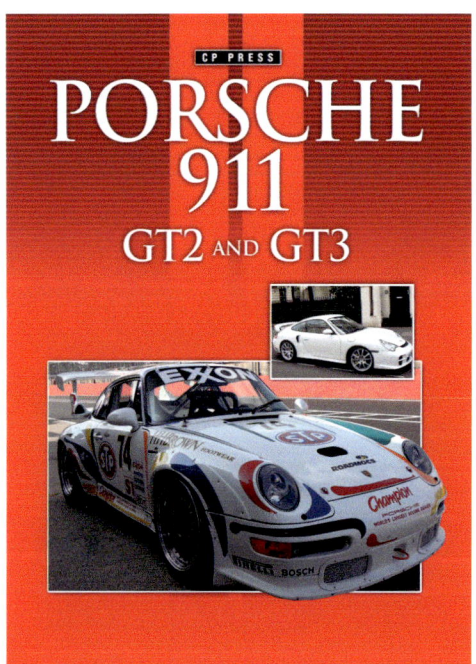

Porsche 911 GT2 and GT3

£14.99

From the first Porsche 993 GT2 through to the latest Porsche 991 GT3 this book looks at all the GT2 and GT3 models that Porsche produced.

- **76 pages softback**
- **255 x 195mm**
- **106 b/w and colour illustrations**
- **ISBN 978-1-910241-08-0**